THE CONVENTIONEERS' GUIDE TO ELIGIBILIZING

BIDEN HARRIS OBAMA

By

Gregory Cliveden

ACTUAL
B
I
D
E
N (44)

ACTUAL
T
R
U
M
P (45)

(No VP)
ERZATZ (46)

TABLE OF CONTENTS

MINUTES REGARDING
THE CONVENTIONEERS' GUIDE
TO ELIGIBILIZING BHO

The Meeting was called to Order by the Chairman, whose name shall not be disclosed to prevent retaliation by the Parties' Forces Contraire ("PFCs"), but to be recorded by Gregory Cliveden, who shall be authorized to cause these minutes to be published as a part of *The Conventioneers' Guide to Eligibilizing BHO*, if, and in whatever manner he deems most appropriate to the purposes established herein, subject to his avoiding any disclosures that may permit said retaliation against anyone participating in these proceedings, or otherwise connected with *The Conventioneers' Guide to Eligibilizing BHO*, or either of the two prior *Guides*, being *The Conventioneers' Guide to Cruzing*

Hillaryously Over Trump, and *The Conventioneers' Guide to the Party at the End of Its Universe*, each available from Amazon.

First Participant: "Bo? Isn't that the name of former President Barack Obama's dog, a Portuguese Water Dog, that lived in the White House at least a few years until Obama's end?"

Chairman: "Wrong on two Counts. First Count: Bo is not a part of the name of our forthcoming book. Second Count: Obama is not a "former President," since he has never been President. The latter was detailed in *The Conventioneers' Guide to Cruzing Hillaryously Over Trump*, and *The Conventioneers' Guide to the Party at the End of Its Universe*, which I recommend you read if you already haven't.

"Further as to the First Count: B, H, and O are the last name initials of Biden, Harris, Obama, and referencing them crunched together. They are the ones needing eligibilizing, not Bo, even though under the circumstances, I suppose, Bo should not actually have been described as the Official White House Pet. However, Bo's status will become legitimized too by the B-H-O eligibilization; posthumously, since Bo died in May, 2021. No need to revise his headstone if the eligibilization occurs. Hopefully, no one would deface it in either event since he is not responsible for, nor even privy to the fraud that was perpetrated and should not be held so. Let BO rest in peace, not so much BHO.

"But you are not alone. Almost everyone got it wrong, many intentionally, even calling the truth 'racism' as revealed in the following which should follow all the intending wrongdoers throughout their lives in infamy until they admit their error and publicly repent, or go to their graves unrepentant, and, presumably, hence to the Everlasting Bonfire that is Hell. That should include the anonymous bloke who authored this following piece about the 2020 Presidential Election. We rely on Gregory to bracket asides and other comments where he deems appropriate so to avoid the piece having any false credence by its publication in The Guide.

> "'President Donald Trump says he has *heard* Democratic candidate Kamala Harris *doesn't qualify* to serve as US vice-president,

amplifying a *fringe* legal theory critics decry as racist. [***Ahem: It's not a 'fringe' legal theory, but rather it is a Constitutional Requirement that definitely has nothing to do with race.***]

"'She was born in the US to a Jamaican father and an Indian mother in Oakland, California, on 20 October 1964. As such, she is eligible to serve as president or vice-president. [***Wrong, as her Father was not a US Citizen at the time of her birth. Hence, she is not a 'natural born Citizen' as required by Article I, Section 1, paragraph 5 of the US Constitution even though a citizen as a result of her birth in the United States.***]

"'For years, Mr. Trump promoted a false *birther* theory that ex-President Barack Obama was not born in the US. [***Ahem: That one be born in the US jurisdiction is One of the Two parts of the Vattel 'natural born Citizen'***] *definition as understood and used by the Founding Fathers in drafting the Constitutional provision regarding qualific-ation to be the President of the United States, and they incor-porated into the Constitution to prevent foreign takeover and to preclude foreign influ-ence in the Presidency and in the Executive Branch.*

"Obama's paternal grand-mother claims her grandson Barack was born in Nigeria. Clearly and indisputably, however, Barack's father was a British Citizen. So Obama may not have met either of the two 'natural born Citizen' def-initional criteria; but defin-itely, he did not meet at least the one requiring patrilineal citizenship.]

"Ms. Harris, a California Senator [*sic*--never that, but instead, a US Senator from, and re-presenting California] was named on Tuesday as the first woman of colour to serve as running mate on a main-party US presidential ticket.

"She is deputy to Democratic White House candidate Joe Biden, who will challenge Mr. Trump, a Republican, in November's general election.

"'The VP has the same eligibility requirements as the president,' Juliet Sorensen, a law professor at Northwestern University, told the Associated Press (AP) news agency.

"'Kamala Harris, she has to be a natural-born Citizen **[but she is not!]**, at least 35 years old, and a resident in the United States for at least 14 years. She is **[not]**. That's really the end of the inquiry.'" *[Ahem: Yes, that is the end of the inquiry. Because she is not a 'natural born Citizen', all the rest is irrelevant. Kamala is not a 'natural born Citizen' solely because her Daddy was not a US citizen at the time of her* *birth. Therefore she is dis-qualified. That is the real the end of the inquiry!*]

'"Anyone born in the US and subject to its jurisdiction is a 'natural born Citizen', regardless of the citizenship of their parents,' says the Cornell Legal Information Institute. [*Wrong because that's not what the Founding Fathers believed they were putting into the Constitution, and did put in.*]

'"The Biden campaign sent a scathing statement in response. 'Donald Trump was the national leader of the grotesque, racist birther movement with respect to President Obama and has sought to fuel racism and tear our nation apart on every single day of his presidency,' a Biden campaign spokesman said in an email. [*So Wrong! And it has nothing to do with racism. The racism argument is an irrational copout for those whose counter-positions have no rational substance. Tagging those who cite the Constitutional meaning of 'natural born Citizen' as grotesque, racist birthers is a gross display of ignorance, and stupidity, if not sheer duplicity. Is it also racist? I believe that it is!* **The racists are calling those who aren't racists.]**

'"So it's unsurprising, but no less abhorrent, that as Trump makes a fool of himself straining to distract the American people from the horrific toll of his failed [**not so**] coronavirus response that his campaign and their allies would resort to wretched, demonstrably false lies in their pathetic desperation.

[*So Wrong!* **So Duplicitous!**]

"What did Trump say?

"After a conservative law professor questioned Ms. Harris' eligibility based on her parents' immigration status at the time of her birth, Mr. Trump was asked about the argument at a press conference.

"The President said: 'I just heard it today that she doesn't meet the requirements and by the way the lawyer that wrote that piece is a very highly qualified, very talented lawyer. I have no idea if that's right. I would have assumed the Democrats would have checked that out before she gets chosen to run for vice-president. But that's a very serious, you're saying that, they're saying that she doesn't qualify because she wasn't born in this country.' [**To be born in the Country is only half of the natural born Citizen requirement. The other half is patrilineal US citizenship, which is the part of the 'natural born Citizen' test that Kamala Devi Harris fails, as well as did Barack Hussein Obama before her.**]

"The reporter replied there was no question that Ms. Harris was born in the US, simply that her parents might not have been permanent US residents at the time.

"Earlier, a Trump campaign adviser, Jenna Ellis, reposted a tweet from the head of conservative group Judicial Watch, Tim Fitton. In that tweet, Mr. Fitton questioned whether Ms. Harris was 'ineligible to be vice-president under the US Constitution's 'citizenship clause'.

"He also shared the opinion piece published in Newsweek magazine by John Eastman, a law professor at Chapman University in California, that Mr. Trump was asked about.

"What is the law professor's argument? Prof Eastman cites Article II of the US Constitution's wording that

> **'no person except a natural born citizen... shall be eligible to the office of president'.**

"He also points out that the 14th Amendment to the Constitution says 'all persons born... in the United States, and subject to the jurisdiction thereof, are citizens.'

"Prof Eastman's argument, which he claims is also being made by other 'commentators', hinges on the idea that Ms. Harris may not have been subject to US jurisdiction if her parents were, for example, on student visas at the time of their daughter's birth in California.

"'Her father was (and is) a Jamaican national, her mother was from India, and neither was a naturalized US citizen at the time of Harris' birth in 1964.' That, according to these commentators, makes her not a 'natural born Citizen' and therefore ineligible for the office of the president and, hence, ineligible for the office of the vice president. **[This is Constitutionally Correct!]**

"In 2010, Prof Eastman ran to be the Republican candidate for California attorney general. He lost to Steve Cooley, who went on to be defeated by Ms. Harris, the Democratic candidate, in the general election.

"Following furious backlash to the Newsweek op-ed, its editor-in-chief Nancy Cooper stood by the decision to publish, arguing on Thursday that Prof Eastman's article had 'nothing to do with racist birtherism' and was instead 'focusing on a long standing, somewhat arcane legal debate'. [*The Constitution and its original meaning are 'arcane legal debate'? Preposterous! And so disrespectful to the Founding Fathers and to Emir de Vattel, the legal scholar from whom the Founding Fathers took the term "natural born Citizen."*]

"What do other constitutional experts say?

"'Berkeley Law School Dean Erwin Chemerinsky told CBS News, the BBC's US partner, that Prof Eastman's argument about

Ms. Harris' eligibility was *truly silly*. [**Chemerinsky is truly silly and therefore not worth countenancing!**]

"He wrote in an email: 'Under section 1 of the 14th Amendment, anyone born in the United States is a United States citizen.' [*Irrelevant. Who is a citizen is not the same as being a "natural born Citizen." Indigenous birth is but one of two aspects of the latter.*]

"'The Supreme Court has held this since the 1890s. Kamala Harris was born in the United States.' [**The Supreme Court was addressing citizenship, not natural born Citizenship fool!**]

"Laurence Tribe, a **[one time]** constitutional law professor at Harvard University and frequent critic of President Trump, also called Prof Eastman's argument '*garbage* and *racist birtherism redux*'. [**Really Wrong!**]

"Jessica Levinson, a professor at Loyola Law School, told AP: 'Let's just be honest about what it is: It's just a racist trope we trot out when we have a candidate of colour whose parents were
not citizens.'
[*Not a racist trope!! It is the Constitution!!! Admittedly, the Constitution does contain language about slavery, but that has nothing to do with the natural born Citizenship issue herein.*

Even were she somehow trans-ported back in time to run as Vice President anytime bet-ween 1788 and 1868 instead of Adams, Jefferson, Burr, Clinton, Gerry, Tompkins, Calhoun, Van Buren, Mentor Johnson, Tyler, Dallas, Fillmore, King, Breckinridge, Hamlin, or Johnson, Harris' skin color, or race would not have been the basis for her rejection. She would have been rejected were she a slave.

She might have been rejected because she was a woman, as not having the right to vote, but not specifically therefor. That disqualification was not eliminated until the 19th Amendment became effective on August 19, 1920. She would have been rejected because she was either not born in the United States, or her Father was not a US Citizen at the time of her birth, the one exception being her having been a US citizen at the time of the adoption of the US Constitution. If she can prove that, all is good! Of course, her incredible age might then raise other questions. Maybe not so much in years in the distant future.]

"How did Trump fuel the Obama *birther* theory?

"Back in 2011, Mr.. Trump began stoking right-wing theories that President Obama might have been born in Kenya.

Even when Mr.. Obama prod-
uced a copy of his birth certificate in April that year showing
he was born in Hawaii, Mr.
Trump continued to claim it was
a *fraud*. **[But so did Obama's
paternal grandmother who
confirmed her grandson was
born in Kenya.]**
"During a September 2016 press
conference, Mr. Trump, then the
Republican White House candidate, was asked about the matter.
He sought to take credit for dis-
peling doubts over Mr. Obama's
eligibility, telling reporters: 'I
finished it. President Obama was
born in the United States.
Period.' **[Irrelevant. Obama's
Father was a British Subject.
Therefore Mr. Obama is not a
natural born Citizen. So
whatever The Donald said,
Obama was not eligible to be
President.]**
"Mr. Trump also argued in 2016
that his Republican rival Ted
Cruz was not eligible to run for

president because he was born in Canada to a US citizen mother and a Cuban-born father." [*True. And what is the relevance of that to the argument about Obama and Harris? Cruz is out on both Counts. He was born in Canada, not a US jurisdiction, and his Father was Cuban, not a US Citizen. As set forth hereinafter, Cruz is not even a US Citizen, and therefore he is not legitimately a US Senator.*]

Participant Two: "We need to find out who is that blithering idiot bloke who wrote that stupid piece so we can tear him apart too."

Participant Three: "The piece does that in itself. So we just did. Why waste our time? Maybe we should contact the law schools at which the named professors teach Constitutional Law and suggest that they might be removed from their posts as unworthy thereof. Tribe is no longer at Harvard. Jessica Levinson is still at Loyola Law School. Juliet Sorensen is still at Northwestern University. Both are so ensconced in their posts that their schools would not be expected to remove them for their false pronouncements about Presidential disqualification."

Gregory Cliveden: "Quite understandably, who is qualified to be President or Vice President usually receives no attention in Law School Constitutional Law classes. So an important question is whether the incorrect opinion of any law professor about Obama and Harris being 'natural born Citizens' should compel their removal from teaching Constitutional Law, indeed, their removal from the faculty altogether. In my opinion, that should not be a foregone conclusion. However, what may be basis for their removal is their lack of scholarship, that is, their lack of research and analysis that such an opinion indicates. At the very least, their law schools should be alerted, as well as those contemplating attending such law schools so that all become informed to make their own decisions about whether educations are advanced by such as these-- Chemerinsky, Levinson, Sorensen."

Participant One: "Let's just see to the distribution of *The Conventioneers' Guide to Eligibilizing BHO*, and let the chips fall where they may. Our goal is reconciliation, not revenge as I see it."

Chairman: "As you are all aware, the issues are these. Biden needs eligibilizing because he has already served two terms as President. That is so because Obama was not eligible to serve as President, the reason being that the Constitution requires the President to be a 'natural born Citizen', which he was not because, even if born in Hawaii, a point disputed by his own paternal grandmother, his father was not a United States citizen, the second prong of the 'natural born Citizen' requirement.

Biden is Constitutionally ineligible to serve a third term because of the 22nd Amendment. Anyone up through Truman could have served more than two terms. Only one did, FDR, who was elected to four, but served only a few months into the last due to his death at 63 from a cerebral hemorrhage."

Participant One: "Which was more definitive and more soon final than the dementia Biden suffers; to complete the comparison betwixt Roosevelt and Biden."

Chairman: "Until then several had tried. They did not get beyond their Party Conventions. One, Teddy Roosevelt, ran under the aegis of a new Party he had created, the Bull Moose Party. In consequence both he and the Republican Candidate, Willian Howard Taft, the Candidate whom Teddy Roosevelt was attempting to replace, lost to that disaster which was Democrat Woodrow Wilson, less than merrily touted as the worst US President of all time."[1]

First Participant: "Hopefully, Trump will not run as the Candidate of another Party in 2024, but if he is not nominated as the Republican Candidate, he may, probably with the same disastrous consequence as for Roosevelt, Taft, and the Country. Another four for Biden. That would rival FDR. No, exceed FDR, at least in age. Sixty-three versus 80."

Second Participant: "The 22nd Amendment provides that 'No person shall be **elected** to the office of the President more than **twice**.' As Biden had never been '**elected** to the office' before 2020, that provision cannot apply to him."

Chairman: "And it mayn't, unless the voters, Electors, Joint Session Sneers knowing of Obama's ineligibility, may be deemed to have been electing Biden as President instead when they were 'electing' a known 'ineligible' as President' together with an 'eligible' Vice President. The provision that definitively applies to him, in any event, is the next following. '…and no person who has held the office of President, or acted as President, for more than two years of a term to which some other person was elected President shall be elected to the office of President more than once.'"

Third Participant: "So arguably under that provision, Biden could serve a 'third term' which would be permitted as his 'once' under that provision of the Constitution. Of course, his second term under Obama could be deemed his 'once' elected. But there again, he was not elected until 2020."

Fourth Participant: "That provision add-resses only one term in which more than two years were served, being no more than four years. Due to Obama's ineligibility for any term, Biden served a second term of four years, never having been 'elected' to that term either, but therefor serving two. Arguably, that second term would con-stitute his second term of more than two years which disqualifies his serving any more. But he was elected only once. In 2020.

That appears from the language of the Constitution to be permitted. So maybe his election in 2020 is Constitutional, albeit his 'once' that precludes him from being re-elected in 2024."

Gregory Cliveden: "Ambiguous at best as that Constitutional provision does not contemplate two terms served in that way. Section 3 of the 20th Amendment must be considered too as it provides another approach to the issue. It provides that 'if the President elect shall have failed to qualify, the Vice President elect shall act as President until a President shall have qualified.' Arguably, that means that Biden was acting as President by virtue of that provision until Trump qualified as President. That provision either has Biden acting a President for two full terms., and not having a third term commencing in 2020, or being within the provision of the 22nd Amendment as one who acted as President more than two years of a term twice in which another was elected, and being thereby precluded from his own term commencing in 2020, as in either scenario, he served eight years, and two terms due to Obama not qualifying."

Chairman: "So the 20th Amendment would seem to be another, perhaps better, basis for Biden's election in 2020 being in violation of the 22nd Amendment."

Gregory Cliveden: "The problem with relying on the 20th Amendment is that **acting as** President is still not the same as being **elected** President. Biden's eight years may be deemed that 'more than two years' but in each of the two terms of the ineligible person who was elected President for purposes of the 22nd Amendment rather than the limiting 'two years of a term' as set forth in the Constitution. Does that permit or prohibit Biden's election in 2020 as that one additional elected term permitted under the 22nd Amendment? At the very least, this situation highlights the ambiguity of the current language of the Constitution. Clearly, the intent was to limit such a former Vice President to one term. So on that basis, Biden would be ineligible for election in 2020. I think both the Originalists and the Tribalists could probably agree on what seems so obvious. Additionally, there is the historical disdain for Presidents serving more than eight years from the outset

27

premised on Washington declining a third term.

FDR's four terms were the reason that the two term limit became a Constitutional limit instead of just a statement by Washington as his reason for not seeking a third term."

First Participant: "Yes, there appears to be room for argument either way as to Biden with respect to term limits under those Amendments."

Chairman: "I think an **election** as Vice President should be deemed an **election** as President when the person **elected** President is ineligibile for the Office. That eliminates all the ambiguity that we have posited here."

Gregory Cliveden: "There is support for that approach in the Original Constitution, being the third paragraph of Section 1 of Article II, which provides that the candidate for President with the second most number of votes for President becomes the Vice President. There was no provision for a separate vote for Vice President until Amendment XII.

"Perhaps the appropriate current resolution would be a Constitutional Amendment adding 'acting as or' wherever 'elected' appears."

First Participant: "Is there any leeway with respect to Obama or Harris under the 'natural born Citizen' requirement?"

Gregory Cliveden: "While the Tribalists assert that 'natural born Citizen' only means that one be born under the jurisdiction of the United States, the Originalists assert that it means, in addition, one must be born of parents who are citizens of the United States, in particular, the father, as that concluded citizenship for wife and children at the time of inclusion of the phrase in the Constitution."

Fourth Participant: "Why do you say Tribalists?"

Chairman: "Because the chief proponent of the concept of the 'living Constitution' is Laurence Tribe, a former Harvard Law Professor, who asserts that the meaning of the Constitution should change with the times. It is in opposition to the Originalist concept that meanings remain the same as at the time of their incorporation by the drafters into the Constitution."

Participant Four: "The Tribalist concept appears to be a clear violation of the provisions of the Constitution for amendment of the Constitution!"

Participant One: "Absolutely!!!"

Participant Four: "Under the Tribalist concept, nothing is absolute. It is whatever Laurence Tribe thinks it should be based on whatever analysis he posits. So Tribe is at least as sanctimonious as was Woodrow Wilson. We can only hope that his sanctimony does not lead to the disasters that President Wilson caused!"

Participant One: "Amen!!!"

Chairman: "As set forth, Gregory, in both of your prior *Conventioneers' Guides*, 'natural born Citizen' was defined by the legal treatise upon which the Founding Fathers relied for the definition of that term, Emer de Vattel's *Les Droit de Gens ou principes de la Loi Naturelle,* which had been translated into English as *The Law of Nations.*"[2]

Gregory Cliveden: "Yes, that is correct. However, not included in those *Guides,* Chairman, were Benjamin Franklin's statements that Vattel's book, in its English translation, was in the hands of the drafters of the Constitution and consulted by them in their drafting. In support of that, Vattel is referenced numerous times in Farrand's Records of the Constitutional Convention (vol. I, pp. 638, 641, 644; and the law of

Nations throughout (vol. I, pp. 58, 471-2, 651;
vol. II, pp. 123, 140, 210, 255, 272, 450, 458,
832, 863, 889, 946; vol. III, 70, 330, 434, 847,
887, 1550, 1615.) So, as I asserted in those
prior *Guides*, the Founding Fathers were
well familiar with the meaning of the term
'natural born Citizen' when they put it into
the Constitution as a requirement for
election to the Presidency to include US
parent citizenry. That assertion is supported by a number of Originalist Constitutional Scholars who are cited in the
prior *Guides*.

"I should add to your statement about Tribe
being the chief proponent of the Living
Constitution. Although he may be such
currently, there have been others. For
example, Justice Brennan, who asserted "We
current Justices read the Constitution in the only
way that we can: as twentieth century Americans.
We look to the history of the time of framing and to
the intervening history of interpretation. But the
ultimate question must be: What do the words of the
text mean in our time? For the genius of the
Constitution rests not in any static meaning it might
have had in a world that is dead and gone, but in the
adaptability of its great principles to cope with
current problems and current needs."[3]

Chairman: Well, you should include that, as well as Franklin's statements in your third *Guide*, the creation of which is the ultimate purpose of our meeting. In your first *Guide* you analyzed Obama's ineligibility, and, after examining all of the actions Obama took as the illegitimate President, concluded 'what did it matter?' parroting former Candidate Hillary Clinton's infamous rhetorical question when asked about Benghazi."

Participant One: "Excepting only Pardons, all of which are invalid according to the appendix included with that *Guide*."

Participant Two: "And excepting also his executive orders. I don't recall whether that is stated in the prior *Guides*. Not sure how many Orders he issued, nothing like the number that Biden had issued already in the first few days of his ersatz third term as President; all of which are null and void too like Obama's, I would suppose."

Participant Four: "Gregory, your analysis of legislation Obama signed seemed a bit dicey. The first *Guide* deemed the legislation effective only because if it were **not** signed by the President, it would become effective merely by the failure to sign after a period of time."

Participant Two: "And if the assertion now is that Biden was President during those times, how does his not having signed that legislation affect that prior conclusion?"

Gregory Cliveden: "All to be analyzed in the third *Guide*, but basically, Biden's not signing has no effect other than as stated in that first *Guide*. Whoever was President, not signing renders the legislation passed per the Constitutional provision to that effect. Those bills that Obama signed are in a different category, however. Insofar as his signing may be deemed fraudulent, the bills that he signed may not have become law. Alternatively, those bills may be deemed to have effect on the same basis as for bills not signed by the President. Everyone faced with the consequences of such 'laws' may have fraud as a basis for challenging the application of such 'laws' to them. Many of those challengeable laws were listed for that purpose in a prior Guide appendix."

Participant Four: "Seems to me the analysis counsels a President to never sign any legislation so to assure its passage despite whatever disability or ineligibility may be claimed against the President."

Gregory Cliveden: "True, but Presidents will probably ignore that counsel always to lay claim to every piece of legislation during their term as their own achievement, their own legacy."

Chairman: "Although Obama's ineligibility made no difference in the 2016 contest between Hillary and The Donald, it should have made a dispositive difference in the 2020 contest between Biden and Trump in favor of Trump."

Participant One: "Had Pence not ignored the analysis and course of action set forth in Gregory's second *Guide*."

Chairman: "Yes. Trump would have continued as President facially as well as actually. But now we are faced with a person purporting to be President who is not, and a purported Vice President, as well, who is not, and who is also therefor ineligible to assume the Office of President should that become necessary."

Participant Two: "It is my understanding that Gregory sent the message to Pence, as well as to all the Congressmen and Senators, and to others who could have influenced

Pence.[4] That should be included in the third
Guide so to shame all those who accepted the
Electors' Unconstitutional Vote for Biden
and Harris who were Constitutionally
Disqualified, Biden because he had already
served two terms due to Obama's
ineligibility; Harris, for the same reason as
Obama: She is not a natural born Citizen!"
Participant One: "Chief Justice Roberts
swore in Joe Biden. He declined to preside
at Trump's Second Impeachment Trial. I
recognize that 'swearing in' the President is
traditional rather than Constitutional,
whereas his presiding over impeachment of
a President is mandated by the Constitution; but his two acts do appear consistent
with Biden being President and Trump not
continuing as President. Do they actually
constitute a correct and judicial determination that Biden is President and Trump
not?"
Gregory Cliveden: "Chief Justice Roberts'
actions should definitely be analyzed in the
third *Guide*, but what a Chief Justice does
beside deciding cases does not constitute a
judicial decision, and has no judicial
precedential value. Currently, I am not
aware that anyone could have had standing

to enjoin a Chief Justice from swearing in anyone. And since no one did, I would be inclined to just leave it at that, put it into Hillary's Bengazi 'what difference does it make' category without spending much time with it in the third *Guide*. But, of course, no one could effectively enjoin a Chief Justice from doing anything as such. So that is not a strong argument, and adds nothing to the analysis."

Participant Three: "According to *Wikipedia*, 15 Chief Justices, one Associate Justice, four Federal Judges, two New York State Judges, and one Notary Public have administered the presidential oath; Presidents sworn in by others than Chief Justices: George Washington, Millard Fillmore, Calvin Coolidge, and Lyndon Johnson."

Participant Two: "That doesn't add up."

Participant One: "There is an intriguing conundrum created by Biden's ineligibility for a third term and the Chief Judge's declining to preside at Trump's Second Impeachment Trial. Since Biden is ineligible for a third term because of Obama's ineligibility, and therefore not President, Trump is President because, unlike the Obama-Biden circumstance, Harris is ineligible to take Biden's place because she too is ineligible for the same reason as Obama: neither is a 'natural born Citizen.' If Trump is President, Chief Justice Roberts was required by the Constitution to preside over Trump's Second Impeachment Trial."

Participant Two: "Add to that, Roberts not doing so renders Trump's Second Impeachment Trial presided over by Democrat Senator Patrick Leahy a nullity."

Gregory Cliveden: "Trump was acquitted. So that Second Impeachment Trial is an absolute nullity for that reason alone. Therefore, it is of no concern in our *Guide* analysis."

Participant Three: "And the situation will continue to exist over the entire time that Biden and Harris hold office as fake President and fake Vice President."

Participant Four: "And beyond too, because if Trump runs for President in 2024, he could be precluded for the same reason Biden should have been in 2020. It would be unconstitutional for Trump to be elected to a third term."

Chairman: "All the more reasons to take the steps necessary to eligibilize Biden, Harris and Obama by the Republicans as well as by the Democrats because that eliminates any impediments, real or imagined to Trump's accession in 2024."

Participant Four: "Both Parties should want that because it benefits both. So what needs to be done?"

Chairman: "As I analyze it, the term 'natural born Citizen' must be changed, and the two term limit must be too. Each will require amendment of the Constitution. Does anyone disagree?"

Gregory Cliveden: "I think only the 'natural born Citizen' provision must be changed. Of course, to effect the eligibilization, it must be made retroactive to a date prior to Obama's election. That solves the problem as to Biden's third term, and Harris' ineligibility. It renders Trump's second Impeachment Trial legal without Roberts presiding, and it permits Trump to run for an unquestionable term as President in 2024."

Participant Two: "Add to that, the unlikelihood of getting enough votes to remove the two term limitation."

Gregory Cliveden: "If the 'natural born Citizen' provision is changed retroactively, the two term limit becomes irrelevant as to Biden and Trump. So no need for eliminating the two term limit? Although others might deem elimination of the two term limit to solve the problem alone, I do not believe so. The ineligibility by virtue of not being a 'natural born Citizen' has to be addressed. While eliminating the two term limit alone may resolve Biden being President and Trump becoming President in 2024, and moots Obama's ineligibility, it does not resolve Harris' ineligibility. Her being eligible would be critical were Biden to become incapacitated, which is likely given his age and apparent cognitive state, or were she to become a candidate for President in 2024. However, eliminating the two term limit as well would permit Obama and Trump to punch it out in 2024."

Chairman: "So should Gregory just concentrate on the one or both?"

Participant One: "I think both are best. However, one or the other would be better than the current situation."

Gregory Cliveden: "I cannot disagree with that. I suspect all here don't either. It would also make Obama eligible for 2024, putting the two most popular and controversial Candidates of recent time head-to-head. I suspect, however, there are many who do not want the problems of the current situation to be brought to public view, and a whole lot more who are totally ignorant of the situation and its impact on future elections, as well as on many, if not most, issues that will arise in the future with respect to the Constitution and Laws passed and signed during these next four years."

Participant Four: "I understand your flagging Laws signed because of Biden's ineligibility, but why do you flag Laws passed without his signing by operation of the Constitutional provision therefor?"

Gregory Cliveden: "The legitimacy of Laws passed with an ineligible Vice President Harris presiding might be subject to challenge in general; but what I had specifically in mind were Laws passed where a tie vote of the Senators was broken by Harris. That would definitely call into question the legitimacy of that Law."

Participant Four: "I see. And this is a real problem with the Senate evenly split between Democrat and Republican votes currently."

Chairman: "So is it agreed that the third *Guide* go forward on all cylinders."

All Participants: "Agreed."

Chairman: "So Gregory get started. Keep us posted by distributing drafts from time to time unto the final. If you need any help of any kind from us, financial, legal, research, anything else, do not hesitate to ask and we shall provide as usual."

Gregory Cliveden: "Reminds me. My favorite *maître de* from an old setting asked when he discovered me at his new, "Your usual?" instead of the "What'll you have?" I anticipated..

Fourth Participant: "Interrupting, reminds me of Biden's gate: 'Waddle you have!"

Gregory Cliveden: "To continue. Not knowing what to expect, not wanting to embarrass the *maître de* or me in front of my tablemates, and whatever the result being within my tolerance for adventure, I said "yes." And he brought me as my pre-prandial a dirty vodka martini up, which I did not remember ever ordering from him, or, indeed, ever having before. However, that did become my go to cocktail thereafter with those tablemates and others there- after. Going with the flow has its benefits!"

Chairman: "Except going with the flow in these circumstances would mean ignoring

Biden's and Harris' ineligibility. We cannot permit that. No one should. It is unconstitutional. What we can do certainly is provide you requisite support. Meeting is adjourned."

THESE ARE THE PROBLEMS

If Biden won the Presidency by Popular Vote, and by Electoral College Vote, what is the problem, you ask. While his winning has been disputed by all the Trumps, by Rudy Giuliani, by Sidney Powell, and by numerous others in ever increasing numbers on the ground of fraudulent paper ballot stuffing, Obama is the definitive fraud most easily discovered and verified. Because Obama is not a 'natural born Citizen' as required by Article II, clause five of the Constitution, the person elected as Vice President contemporaneously with him becomes the President, and remains such until an eligible person is elected President. That happened next when Trump was elected. Trump is the one who replaced Biden as President after Biden's eight year two term Presidency due to the ineligibility of Obama.

How Biden became President under the Constitution in 2020 creates one problem.

That would not be a problem were it not for the 22nd Amendment which limits a President to two terms. Nor would it be a problem if the 'natural born Citizen' requirement had not existed to render Obama ineligible to become President.

Both of those problems can be eliminated by repealing the 22nd Amendment retroactive to a time before Biden's inauguration as President on January 2020, and changing the 'natural born Citizen' requirement to a time before Obama's initial inauguration on January 20, 2009. Of course, tandem retro-activity to the earlier date would eliminate the 2020 problem for Biden, and also eliminate any question about the *bona fides* of another term for Obama in 2024, which might be the path preferred by the Democrats given all the current questions about Biden's mental state, and Harris' repeated silly giggling.

Repeal of a Constitutional provision has never been made to a prior date. Repeal of Prohibition was prospective. Arguably, the Bill of Rights was retrospective from the ten amendments constituting its adoption by the States on 12/15/1791 to the date of the adoption of the Constitution itself on

6/21/1788, or at least to the date of adoption of the Bill of Rights by the House of Representatives on 8/21/1789.

However, the Bill of Rights remained essentially unutilized for more than 130 years after adoption, when the States were first deemed to be subject to its edicts via the 14th Amendment. See *Now Cherished, Bill of Rights Spent a Century in Obscurity*, published 12/12/2019 on *uscourts.gov*.

Prospective repeal of the 22nd Amendment would aid only Trump in the scenario, if he even needs it. And whether he needs it is dependent on whether he is still President currently because Biden's inauguration was for an unconstitutional third term.

Even though retroactive passage has never been done before, there is no prohibition in the Constitution. The *ex post facto* prohibition in the Constitution applies to Laws passed by Congress. The Constitution is definitely a Law. Congress is involved in proposing Amendments, or implementing the process when the State Legislatures do the proposing. However, such Amendments are passed by the States, not by the Congress. That should mean that there is no prohibition against an Amendment to the

Constitution having retrospective application.

If the 22nd Amendment is not repealed, Biden may be deemed serving an unconstitutional third term. That would leave eligibilizing Obama's Presidency as the sole means of solving Biden's third term problem. Eligibilizing Obama's Presidency requires elimination or redefinition of the 'natural born Citizen' requirement. Doing that would also eligibilize Kamala Harris' Vice Presidency. Democrats might deem that most efficacious therefor.

No one would espouse eliminating 'natural born Citizen' from the list of Presidential requirements entirely because that would permit anyone 35 and older who had resided in the United States for at least 14 years at any non-contiguous time to become President no matter what their citizenship or allegiance elsewhere.

The answer must be to redefine the phrase 'natural born Citizen' so to eliminate the patrilineal citizenship requirement of its Original definition. The best means of doing that is by substituting that phrase with another which does not have the natural born restriction. The easiest substitute would be the one that the Tribalists assert as the evolved current meaning of the phrase in the Constitution. That would be "anyone born in the jurisdiction of the United States" without regard to parentage.

As with elimination of the third term requirement, permitting anyone born in the jurisdiction of the United States to be President or Vice President might prove too unpopular for passage by 2/3rds of Congress or 3/4ths of the States. It would include the child of any woman who slipped ever so briefly into the jurisdiction to give birth to her child. It could include children of foreign diplomats, foreign students as is the case with Barack Obama and Kamala Harris, foreign visitors, temporary foreign vacationers, temporary foreign workers, other types unknown, including the current pregnant illegal aliens crashing the Southern Border. If not already, such a journey could become a common practice among the other Nations to effect their ace-in-the-hole for their seeding every future Presidential election.

As there is no continuity requirement for residency in the Constitution, all foreigners whose mothers slipped into the United

States ever so briefly to effect their birth here, and who resided in the United States for any non-contiguous times so to equal fourteen years of residency in their 35 or more years would qualify to become President even though they could have spent most of their lives elsewhere, being groomed and otherwise indoctrinated to do another Country's bidding.

Better also to substitute "person" for "anyone" so as to preclude the Republicans from electing their elephant. Admittedly, that's irrelevant for the Democrats since donkeys do not live long enough to survive into the 35 year age limit currently. The Democrats would have to opt for a mule instead if they did not want to change their look too much. A mule surviving into a second term would be unlikely, however, so changing the Party's appearance by substituting a tortoise would make the Democrats competitive with the Republicans. Only problem, of course, is that the long lived tortoise is so slow moving throughout its life; visibly on land, not so much invisibly at sea, perhaps. Perfect fit all around therefor, given that cognition does not seem to be an issue currently for the Democrats who may be deemed biden at sea? [Check this with the Board before including.][√] Perhaps, but that change is even more unlikely than repealing the 22nd Amendment. Distinguishing between "any- one" and "any person" may be too pedantic for consideration. But why take a chance given the current inattentiveness to the details of qualifications such as competence and eligibility, as evidenced by Biden's ascension, and Harris' selection.

HOW TO FIX THE PROBLEMS. AND HOW LIKELY

Eliminating the two term limit of the 22nd Amendment may be accomplished by either of the two methods set forth in Article V of the Constitution.

> **Article V:** The Congress, whenever two thirds of both houses shall deem it necessary, shall propose amendments to this Constitut- ion, or, on the application of the legislatures of two thirds of the several states, shall call a con- vention for proposing amend- ments, which, in either case, shall

be valid to all intents and purposes, as part of this Constitution, when ratified by the legislatures of three fourths of the several states, or by conventions in three fourths thereof, as the one or the other mode of ratification may be proposed by the Congress; provided that no amendment which may be made prior to the year one thousand eight hundred and eight shall in any manner affect the first and fourth clauses in the ninth section of the first article; and that no state, without its consent, shall be deprived of its equal suffrage in the Senate.

Currently, the Senate is essentially evenly split between Republican and Democrat votes (48 Republicans, 48 Democrats, plus 3 generally Democratically aligned Independents, one vacancy), the Vice President having the Constitutional power to break ties in her role as President of the Senate; the House 48.85% Democrats and 51.15% Republicans of 434 Representatives due to one current vacancy [Source: *Wikipedia*.]

So currently, 289 Representatives and 67 Senators would have to vote for amendment, assuming "2/3rd of both Houses" actually means 2/3rds of **each** House. Otherwise, 356 total votes could propose the Amendment irrespective of whether the votes of Senators or Representatives. But assuming straight Party voting, in the Senate: 48 Democrats, 48 Republicans, 3 Independents who usually align with the Democrats, one vacancy; in the House Republicans 222, Democrats 212, one vacancy, meaning neither Party alone could propose the Amendment without substantial help from the other.

However, since the Amendment would benefit both Democrats and Republicans, because it eligibilizes Biden, and preserves another run at the Presidency for Trump even were he deemed to be President during 2020-2024, both Party's Members may be expected to vote to propose it to the States, more so Biden than Trump. The obvious impediment is that elimination of the two term limit would also apply beyond the immediate outcome and permit persons to be President forever, just like the Vice President, which office has no current term

limitation.[5] Of course, the mid-term election in 2022 could have made the Amendment
possible based solely on the votes of one
Party or the other. However, that did not
happen even with all those immigrants
crashing the border at the invitation of Biden
as they could not be granted citizenship in
time for the 2022 election, and even Biden's
miserable performance, coupled with Harris'
giggling were not sufficient to sweep out the
Democrats and replace them with enough
Republicans.

An Amendment to eliminate the two term
limit would require the Parties to join
together to effect it. Given the mutual
benefit, that is possible if the Party Members are educated to understand the mutual
benefit. Presumably, this book may aid in
that effort.

However implemented, the Amendment
could look like this:

AMENDMENT XXVIII

The twenty second article of amendment to
the Constitution of the United States is
hereby repealed retrospective to [January
20, 2009][6] upon this provision's ratification

as an amendment to the Constitution by the legislatures of three-fourth of the several States by November 5, 2024.

Changing 'natural born Citizen' to 'a person born in the jurisdiction of the United States' might be more possible than eliminating the prohibition against more than two terms, given the historical disdain for Presidents serving more than eight years. Even though it does not address the Founding Fathers' and Originalists' concern for loyalty by requiring patrilineal citizenry, birth within the jurisdiction and at least 14 years of contiguous residency within the jurisdiction may be sufficiently comforting. After all, it was sufficient for Obama, who was allegedly born in Hawaii, of a US Citizen mother, and of a British Subject father who met as students in the US, and for Harris, who was born in California, of a Citizen of India mother, and of a British Subject father, who too met as students in the US. The comfort level may be expected to increase exponentially as the US citizenry becomes ever more based on mere birth in the jurisdiction as a result of illegals pouring through US' open borders under the Biden

Administration's promise to grant them all citizenship.

Changing 'natural born Citizen' to 'Citizen' is another possibility. After all, that is sufficient for every other office than President and Vice President.

The difference between these offices and all others is that the personal prerogatives and powers of the President are so much more than any other office that additional measures to assure loyalty must have been deemed essential by the Founding Fathers.

Without parental loyalty, the child's loyalty cannot be expected. Likewise with local birth, although that alone is much less certain, especially if the parents entered illegally and therefore without any proper vetting.

The process toward citizenship by naturalization may assure more loyalty than citizenship by birth absent the additional requirement of patrilineal citizenship. That seems obvious. However, currently a naturalized citizen is precluded from the Presidency. Why is that? The only explanation must be that birth in the jurisdiction of parents who are citizens was deemed of paramount importance to assuring enduring loyalty to the US.

Can these uncertainties be overlooked on the premise that voters know the specific individuals whose ineligibility we are attempting to eliminate? That is not to say that there have never been concerns about the loyalties of Obama and Harris to the US during the courses of their lives. After all, both lived considerable times of their lives elsewhere, Obama in the Philippines under the tutelage of a Philippine step-father; Harris with her mother in Canada. She claims her Indian grandfather had sub-stantial influence over her. Of course, an amendment must look not just to them but to those yet unknown in circumstances yet unknowable.

Eliminating the birth requirement would permit anyone who ever resided within the jurisdiction of the US for a total of 14 years to become President or Vice President. Merely requiring Citizenship would permit a 14 year resident to be inaugurated immediately following the naturalization ceremony. Would this be acceptable? I doubt it.

However, to become a US Representative one has only to have been a citizen for seven years; to become a Senator only nine. There is no requirement that a Justice of the Supreme Court, nor any other federal judge meet any age, citizenship or residency requirement, nor even have a law degree. In fact, 49 of the 114 Supreme Court Justices did not have law degrees; but that includes the early years when one became a lawyer by apprenticing to a practicing lawyer.

Of course, the results of the mid-term election in 2022 could have made Amendment eliminating the birth requirement possible retrospectively as the Party in the majority (currently the Democrat Party) usually loses its majority to the Party in the minority (currently the Republican Party) at mid-term; but it didn't in the Senate due to three Independents who generally align with the Democrats; nor in the House of Representatives.

The other resolution is to ignore the Vattel meaning of 'natural born Citizen,' declaring it not vital, and adopting the Tribalist meaning in its stead. (No reference to systemic racism intended.) In effect, of course, that is what permitted Obama and

Harris to be elected. That would require nothing more, perhaps, than figuratively, or literally, burning Vattel's Law of Nations, Farrand's Records of the Constitutional Convention, and whatever Ben Franklin and other Founding Founders may have said *ex tempore* can be found. Perhaps, the Constitution too? Cancel Culture!

Why even that? After all, these historical references can just be ignored, just as they have been ignored currently. They need not be acted upon. After all, ignorance and inaction are not actionable in our culture despite the damage they cause unless one can be charged with the duty to know or to act.

Furthermore, Book Burnings' reprehensible history may be sufficient shield against burning those essential historical, living documents however. [See Wikipedia-*Book Burning*.] Supporters of the original meaning of the Constitution may be cowed into silence merely by facetious accusations that their reliance on the original meaning of the Constitution is "truly silly," or a "fringe legal theory," as some self-aggrandizing *faux* "truly silly" legal [???] scholars [???] have already asserted. For which see, pp. 2-6 above, and Cliveden's *The Conventioneers' Guide to the Party at the End of Its Universe*, also available on Amazon. The Originalists might even be cowed into silence for fear of being attacked as racists based on their support of the actual language of the Constitution, which did make provision for slavery, as well as gender subordination.

However implemented, the Amendment could look like this:

AMENDMENT XXIX

The fifth paragraph of Section 1 of Article II of the Constitution of the United States is hereby amended retrospective to [January 20, 2009][7] upon ratification of this amendment to the Constitution by the legislatures of three-fourth of the several States by November 5, 2024 as follows:

No Person except a Person born in the jurisdiction of the United States shall be eligible to the Office of President; neither shall any Person be eligible to that Office who shall not have attained to the Age of thirty-five Years, and been fourteen Years a Resident within the United States.

Changing the residency provision to require it be "within the United States immediately preceding election" might be a good idea too in order to eliminate the possibility of meeting the requirement piecemeal as now. Thus:

No Person except a Person born in the jurisdiction of the United States shall be eligible to the Office of President; neither shall any Person be eligible to that Office who shall not have attained to the Age of thirty-five Years, and been fourteen Years a Resident continuously within the jurisdiction of the United States immediately preceding such election.

The 'within the jurisdiction' language accommodates those Citizens beyond the borders but still subject to United States' jurisdiction; soldiers and diplomatic corp. personnel, for example.

The fifth paragraph of Section 1 of Article II of the Constitution of the United States also provided that "...a Citizen of the United States, at the time of the adoption of this Constitution shall be eligible to the Office of the President." This may be deleted as no longer necessary. However, it is important historically as an adjunct to the meaning of the immediately preceding 'natural born Citizen' phrase. Such exception had to be made to permit Washington and others following through Jackson to be eligible for the Presidency; Van Buren being the first to be born a United States Citizen rather than a British Subject, whose Dad, Abraham was also born in the United States. So Van Buren was the first President who was eligible as a 'natural born Citizen' rather than as 'a Citizen of the United States, at the time of the adoption of the Constitution' as were the seven before him.

So the Originalists might want to retain that provision in the Constitution. Combined with Vattel, it gives historical support for their position as to the original meaning of 'natural born Citizen' intended by the Founding Fathers. Presumably, the Tribalists would want it eliminated so to obfuscate the historical support for the meaning of 'natural born Citizen' in the Constitution on the premise that historical meaning is no longer relevant for a living Constitution which should owe its meaning solely to current times, even though the Tribalists' seeking such an amendment would be thereby contradicting their own 'amendments be damned' posture as unnecessary posturing.

Removing Biden from Office.

As amending the Constitution timely seems unlikely absent joint Party participation even though such an amendment would appear to be in the best interest of both Parties, there are two legitimate methods that may be utilized to remove the ineligible Biden. They are removal under the 25th Amendment to the Constitution, and the Constitution's Impeachment Clauses.
The 25th Amendment provides in pertinent part as follows when the President does not acquiesce to his own removal, the prior Sections [1 through 3 thereof] setting forth the procedure when he does acquiesce.

Amendment XXV

Section 4. Whenever the Vice President and a majority of either the principal officers of the executive departments, or of such other body as Congress may by law provide,[8] transmit to the President *pro tempore* of the Senate and the Speaker of the House of Representatives their written declaration that the President is unable to discharge the powers, and duties of his office, the Vice President shall immediately assume the powers and duties of the office as Acting President.

Thereafter, when the President transmits to the President *pro tempore* of the Senate and the Speaker of the House of Representatives his written declaration that no inability exists, he shall resume the powers and duties of his office unless the Vice President and a majority of either the principal officers of the executive department or of such other body as Congress may by law provide, transmit within four days to the President *pro tempore* of the Senate and the Speaker of the House of Representatives their written declaration that the President is unable to discharge the powers and duties of his office. Thereupon Congress shall decide the issue, assembling within forty-eight hours for that purpose if not in session. If the Congress, within twenty-one days after receipt of the latter written declaration, or, if Congress is not in session, within twenty-one days after Congress is required to assemble, determines by two-thirds vote of both Houses that the President is unable to discharge the powers and duties of his office, the Vice President shall continue to discharge the same as Acting President; Otherwise, the President shall resume the powers and duties of his office.

How likely is that scenario to play out against Biden? The preliminary process is all within the province of the Democrat Party, the Vice President and all the executive officers being Democrats. The hang-up could be the two-thirds vote of both Houses. That it is two-thirds instead of three-fourths does make it more possible, however.

In this process, presumably, most of the members of both the Senate and the House would vote that Biden is unable if the Democrat Vice President and the Democrat executive officers are the ones presenting the issue to Congress. But is that presentation unlikely if the general surmise is true, being that Biden is a demented puppet controlled by his executive officers anyway? If so, why would a majority of them vote with Kamala Harris to put her in charge, especially given the ineffectiveness of her charges currently, and her continuing public gaffes and giggling?

Therefor, failure to proceed pursuant to Amendment XXV cannot be deemed in any way a determination that Biden is not what he seems, a person who is mentally unqualified to be President.
This lack of qualification is not the primary basis for Biden's removal. This method of removal cannot be a preferred basis for removal either, given that his substitute is also Constitutionally disqualified from being either Vice President or President.

Impeachment.

Clause 5, Section 2, Article I of the Constitution provides in pertinent part:

The House of Representatives...shall have the sole Power of Impeachment.

Clause 6, Section 3, Article I of the Constitution provides:

The Senate shall have the sole Power to try all Impeachments. When sitting for that Purpose, they shall be on Oath or Affirmation. When the President of the United States is tried, the Chief Justice shall preside: And no Person shall be convicted without the Concurrence of two thirds of the Members present.
Before that can happen, of course, the House must file Articles of Impeachment with the Senate.

Article II, Section 4 provides the premises therefor as follows.

Section 4. The President, Vice President and all civil Officers of the United States, shall be removed from Office on Impeachment for, and Conviction of,

Treason, Bribery, or other high Crimes
and Misdemeanors.

Treason and Bribery were sufficiently
defined terms at the time of the drafting the
Constitution. Other high Crimes and
Misdemeanors were not. So they are
amenable to Tribe's approach to Constitutional reinterpretations rather than the
Originalist approach because the latter is too
ambiguous for conclusion or preclusion.

So how to address the impeachment of
Biden and Harris?

Treason--Article III, Section 3 provides in
pertinent part:

> Treason against the United States shall
> consist only in levying War against
> them, or in adhering to their Enemies,
> giving them Aid and Comfort.

That would seem to prelude either Biden or
Harris from being impeached for assuming
offices to which they are not Constitutionally entitled on the ground of
Treason.

A case might be made for Bribery as follows per provision by Congresswoman Margorie Taylor Greene.

"117TH CONGRESS
1ST SESSION

"H. RES. 57

"Impeaching Joseph R. Biden, President of the United States, for abuse of power by enabling bribery and other high crimes and misdemeanors.

"IN THE HOUSE OF REPRESENTATIVES

"JANUARY 21, 2021

"Mrs. GREENE of Georgia submitted the following resolution; which was referred to the Committee on the Judiciary

---

"RESOLUTION

"Impeaching Joseph R. Biden, President of the United States, for abuse of power by enabling bribery and other high crimes and misdemeanors.

"Resolved, That Joseph Robinette Biden, President of the United States, is impeached for abuse of power by enabling bribery and other high crimes and misdemeanors, and that the following article of impeachment be exhibited to the United States Senate:

"Article of impeachment exhibited by the House of Representatives of the United States of America in the name of itself and of the people of the United States of America, against Joseph Robinette Biden, President of the United States of America, in maintenance and support of its impeachment against him for abuse of power by enabling bribery and other high crimes and misdemeanors.

"ARTICLE I: ABUSE OF POWER

"The Constitution provides that the House of Representatives "shall have the sole Power of Impeachment" and that the President "shall be removed from Office on Impeachment for, and Conviction of, Treason, Bribery, or other high Crimes and Misdemeanors.

"In his conduct as the former Vice President and current President of the United States, in violation of his constitutional oath faithfully to execute the offices of the Vice Presidency and President of the United States, and, to the best of his ability, preserve, protect, defend, the Constitution of the United States, and in violation of his constitutional duty to take care that the laws be faithfully executed--Joseph Robinette Biden abused the power of the Office of the Vice President, enabling bribery and other high crimes and mis- demeanors, by allowing his son to influence the domestic policy of a foreign nation and accept various benefits--including financial compensation-- from foreign nationals in ex- change for certain favors.

"As Vice President, Joseph Biden was the senior Obama Administration official over- seeing anti-corruption efforts in Ukraine. Hence, any illegal activity involving corrupt- ion conducted by Hunter Biden within or in relation to Ukraine would fall under the purview of the Office of Vice President Biden and the Obama State Department's anti- corruption efforts. In fact, many State Department officials within the Obama Administration repeatedly registered reservat- ions about Hunter Biden's role on the board of a corrupt company. Thus, any instances of corruption on behalf of Hunter Biden via his role as a board member of the Ukrainian- operated Burisma energy firm were either not investigated or covered up. The evidence of widespread knowledge, corruption, and collusion on behalf of the Biden family with foreign nationals is clear and compelling.

"Among other examples, it has been materially demonstrated that:

"(1) According to the U.S. Senate Committee on Homeland Security and Governmental Affairs and the U.S. Senate Committee on Finance, the Vice President's office and State Department officials were aware but ignored concerns relating to Hunter Biden's role on the board of a Ukrainian-based natural gas company (hereafter, 'Burisma').

"(2) According to the same sources, Hunter Biden's and his family's financial transactions with Ukrainian, Russian, Kazakh, and Chinese nationals raise criminal concerns and extortion threats.

"(3) In early 2015 the former Acting Deputy Chief of Mission at the U.S. Embassy in Kyiv, Ukraine, George Kent, raised concerns to officials in Vice President Joe Biden's office about the perception of a conflict of interest with respect to Hunter Biden's role on Burisma's board. Kent's concerns went unaddressed, and in September 2016, he emphasized in an email to his colleagues, 'Furthermore, the presence of Hunter Biden on the Burisma board was very awkward for all

U.S. officials pushing an anticorruption agenda in Ukraine.'

"(4) In October 2015, senior State Department official Amos Hochstein raised concerns with Vice President Biden, as well as with Hunter Biden, that Hunter Biden's position on Burisma's board enabled Russian disinformation efforts and risked undermining U.S. policy in Ukraine. Vice President Biden did not resolve this conflict of interest. Instead, he enabled it.

"(5) In addition to the over $4 million paid by Burisma for Hunter Biden's board membership, Hunter Biden, and his family received millions of dollars from foreign nationals with questionable backgrounds. Specifically, the ongoing FBI investigation into Hunter Biden's laptop revealed that Hunter received a 2.8 carat diamond gift from a high-ranking Chinese official in 2017. Hunter Biden told the New Yorker Magazine that he 'felt uncomfortable receiving the diamond and gave it to other associates.'

"(6) Hunter Biden had business associations with Ye Jianming, founder of the CEFC China Energy Company, Ltd., Gongwen Dong, and other Chinese nationals linked to the Communist government and the People's Liberation Army. Those associations resulted in millions of dollars in cash flow. There exists a vast web of corporate connections and financial transactions between and among the Biden family and Chinese nationals.

"(7) Hunter Biden paid nonresident women who were nationals of Russia or other Eastern European countries and who appear to be linked to an 'Eastern European prostitution or human trafficking ring.'

"(8) In 2016, Ukraine's top anti-corruption prosecutor, Viktor Shokin, had an active and ongoing investigation into Burisma and its owner, Mykola Zlochevsky. At the time, Hunter Biden continued to serve on Burisma's board of directors. According to news reports, then Vice-President Biden 'threatened to withhold $1 billion in United States loan guarantees if Ukraine's leaders did not dismiss [Shokin].' After that, Ukraine's Parliament fired Shokin.

"(9) Hunter Biden received millions of dollars from foreign sources as a result of business relationships that he built during the period when his father was Vice President of the United States and after. The financial transactions which Hunter engaged in illustrate serious counterintelligence and extortion concerns relating to Hunter Biden and his family.

"(10) Hunter Biden's work with Chinese nationals connected to the Communist regime illustrate the deep financial connections that accelerated while his father was Vice President and continued after he left office.

"(11) On June 23, 2011, Sean Conlon, a business associate of Hunter Biden, suggested that a $10 billion deal could be struck in exchange for certain persons meeting Vice President Biden. This shows deliberate 'pay-for-play' and 'quid-pro-quo.' The email, in full, to Robert Biden, from Sean Conlon, is as follows:

"(A) 'So we have engagement letter if they get other 10 bonds they have a face value of 10b. While it is farfetched Devon [Archer] said he talked to his professor and these get traded. We get 10% in fees. We need to get these guys to an event or something where they get to just formally meet your Dad. For follow on they can talk to Chief of Staff. Let me know how soon we can do that. V brief. If Nagi get that done we get more bonds to move. Regards your hard working partner in Positano! Sean' (emphasis added).

"(12) Emails between Hunter Biden and his cousin reveal that the President of Hunter's Chinese Communist Party-linked firm, Eric Schwerin, repeatedly asked Hunter for an appointment to the Commission for the Preservation of America's Heritage Abroad—a position he ultimately received. The email from Hunter to his cousin, Missy, regarding the request for the appointment to the Commission is as follows:

'(A) Eric asked for one of these [an appointment] the day after the election in 2008. You know better than me what are real and interesting appointments. Let's go through the list with Steve and see what makes sense. I don't know how much 2016 and nepotism plays into it.'

"In all of this, President Biden gravely endangered the security of the United States and its institutions of government. Through blatant nepotism, he enabled his son to influence foreign policy and financially benefit as a result of his role as Vice President. He supported his son engaging in collusion with Chinese Communist Party-linked officials. He allowed his son to trade appointments with his father and other high-ranking administration officials in exchange for financial compensation. He permitted his son to take money from Russian oligarchs, including Elena Baturina, the wife of the former mayor of Moscow.

"In so doing, Joseph R. Biden threatened the integrity of the democratic system, interfered with the peaceful transition of power, and imperiled a coordinate branch of government. He thereby betrayed his trust as former Vice President and current President, to the manifest injury of the people of the United States.

"Wherefore President Biden, by such conduct, has demonstrated that he will remain a threat to national security, democracy, and the Constitution if allowed to remain in office, and has acted in a manner grossly incompatible with self-governance and the rule of law. President Biden thus warrants impeachment and trial, removal from office, and disqualification to hold and enjoy any office of honor, trust, or profit under the United States."

High Crimes and Misdemeanors was substituted by the Founding Fathers for "maladministration," the original phrase under discussion on the ground that "maladministration" was too ambiguous.[9] Unfortunately, this substitution is also ambiguous as the terms High Crimes and Misdemeanors have come to be used in the Constitutional context not to require the commission of a crime *contra* their use in the criminal context, which do.[10]

Mrs. Green has also put forth a further basis for Biden's Impeachment following the Afghan Withdrawal Debacle as follows for 'dereliction of duty.' I would suggest that 'dereliction of duty' smacks too much like 'maladministration' which the Founding Fathers rejected on the ground that the best remedy for that was the requirement of re-election every four years. The better premise for such an impeachment is the following specific language from Article III, Section 3 of the Constitution:

"Treason against the United States shall consist...in adhering to their Enemies, giving them Aid and Comfort."

So these phrases of the Constitution could either be added to 'dereliction of duty' or substituted for it.

In the House of Representatives Mrs. Greene submitted the following resolution:

"117th Congress,
"1st Session

"RESOLUTION

"Impeaching Joseph Robinette Biden, President of the United States, for dereliction of duty[, and adhering to the United States'

Enemies and giving them Aid and Comfort] by leaving behind thousands of American civilians and Afghan allies, along with numerous taxpayer-financed weapons and military equipment, endangering the lives of the American people and the security of the United States. Resolved, that Joseph Robinette Biden, President of the United States, is impeached for dereliction of duty[, **and adhering to the United States' Enemies and giving them Aid and Comfort]**by leaving behind thousands of American civilians and Afghan allies, along with numerous taxpayer-financed weapons and military equipment, endangering the lives of the American people and the security of the United States, and that the following articles of impeachment be exhibited to the United States Senate: Articles of impeachment exhibited by the House of Representatives of the United States of America in the name of itself and of the people of the United States of America, against Joseph Robinette Biden, President of the United States of America, in maintenance and support of its impeachment against him for dereliction of duty[, **and adhering to the United States' Enemies and giving them Aid and Comfort]** by leaving behind thousands of American civilians and Afghan allies, along with numerous taxpayer-financed weapons and military equipment, endangering the lives of the American people and the security of the United States. The Constitution provides that the House of Representatives "shall have the sole Power of Impeachment" and that the President "shall be removed from Office on Impeachment for, and Conviction of, Treason, Bribery, or other high Crimes and Misdemeanors." In his conduct as President of the United States, in violation of his constitutional oath faithfully to execute the office of the President of the United States, and, to the best of his ability, preserve, protect, defend, the Constitution of the United States— Joseph Robinette Biden showed dereliction of duty[, **by adhering to the United States' Enemies and giving them Aid and Comfort]** by leaving behind thousands of American civilians and Afghan allies, along with numerous taxpayer-financed weapons and military equipment, endangering the lives of the American people and the security of the United States.

"ARTICLE I Whereas Joe Biden failed to secure the extraction of thousands of American civilians and Afghan Allies before and during the withdrawal between August 14 and August 16, 2021, putting thousands of lives in imminent danger from the Taliban. Whereas, as Commander-in-Chief, Joe Biden has armed our enemies by leaving numerous weapons, ammunition, and other military equipment which could be used against American citizens, allies, and other civilians in Afghanistan. Whereas Joe Biden has shown the American people that his administration failed to properly prepare for the extraction of civilian and military assets from the nation of Afghanistan. Whereas Joe Biden abandoned tens of thousands of American citizens and Afghan allies stuck in Afghanistan at danger of being captured, tortured, held hostage for ransom, or killed. In each of these actions, Joseph R. Biden showed grave dereliction of duty[, **by adhering to the United States' Enemies and giving them Aid and Comfort]** and continues to demonstrate that he is unfit to hold the office of President of the United States. Wherefore President Biden, by such conduct, has demonstrated that he will remain a threat to national security and the Constitution if allowed to remain in office, and has acted in a manner grossly incompatible with self-governance and the rule of law. President Biden thus warrants impeachment and trial, removal from office, and disqualification to hold and enjoy any office of honor, trust, or profit under the United States."

The Basic Impeachment Conundrum.

The impeachment scenario suffers a basic conundrum. How can one be impeached who does not hold the office from which one is to be removed by the impeachment? The premise here is that neither Biden nor Harris legitimately holds the office of President or Vice President due to each being Constitutionally Ineligible for that office, albeit for the different reasons that Biden cannot serve a third term since only two are permitted by the Constitution, and that Harris is not a 'natural born Citizen' as required by the Constitution.
Are they mere trespassers? If so, what are the remedies? Who the enforcers?   18 USC 1752 provides criminal penalty for those who trespass federal buildings as follows:
"(a)Whoever—"(1) knowingly enters or remains in any restricted building or grounds without lawful authority to do so;
"(2) knowingly, and with intent to impede or disrupt the orderly conduct of Government business or official functions, engages in disorderly or disruptive conduct in, or within such proximity to, any restricted building or grounds when, or so that, such conduct, in fact,

impedes or disrupts the orderly conduct of Government business or official functions;

"**(3)** knowingly, and with the intent to impede or disrupt the orderly conduct of Government business or official functions, obstructs or impedes ingress or egress to or from any restricted building or grounds; or [1]

"**(4)** knowingly engages in any act of physical violence against any person or property in any restricted building or grounds; [2]

***

"**(b)** The punishment for a violation of subsection (a) is—

"**(1)** a fine under this title or imprisonment for not more than 10 years, or both, if—

"**(A)** the person, during and in relation to the offense, uses or carries a deadly or dangerous weapon or firearm; or

"**(B)** the offense results in significant bodily injury as defined by section 2118(e)(3); and

"**(2)** a fine under this title or imprisonment for not more than one year, or both, in any other case.

"**(c)**In this section—

"**(1)**the term "restricted buildings or grounds" means any posted, cordoned off, or otherwise restricted area—

80

"**(A)** of the White House or its grounds, or the Vice President's official residence or its grounds;

"**(B)** of a building or grounds where the President or other person protected by the Secret Service is or will be temporarily visiting; or

"**(C)** of a building or grounds so restricted in conjunction with an event designated as a special event of national significance; and

"**(2)** the term "other person protected by the Secret Service" means any person whom the United States Secret Service is authorized to protect under section 3056 of this title or by Presidential memorandum, when such person has not declined such protection."

Is this not the statute upon which those protesting the certification of illegitimate Electors by Congress on January 6, 2021 are being prosecuted?

So 18 USC 1752 could serve also to remove Biden and Harris from the abodes they are currently occupying on the pretext of being President and Vice President, but that would not effect their removal from their offices which they do not Constitutionally hold. Rather it would be but an adjunct thereto.

Even though their conviction of this crime would provide basis for impeachment were they officeholders, the aforesaid conundrum, i.e. that they are not Constitutionally President and Vice President, prevents that basis.

A sentence of imprisonment would provide a lawful place for them to be, and from which they could continue to pretend to be President and Vice President, respectively. Under the circumstances, a sentence equal to the terms of their offices as President and Vice President would be appropriate. This is possible if the criteria for a sentence of up to 10 years under the 18 USC 1752(b) were met. It is possible, but unlikely, that Biden or Harris were "carrying or using" to meet the criteria for the 10 year sentence. However, there occupation could be deemed to have resulted in significant bodily injury due to their various actions and neglects, particularly in Afghanistan and at the Southern Border, potentially in whatever either does or does not do upon a Russian invasion of Ukraine. Otherwise, the sentence would only be one year.

The significant bodily injury resulting from the misnamed January 6 Insurrection might not be deemed to count toward a Biden and Harris sentence enhancement because that event did not occur during their trespass, even though the processing of the Electoral Votes in Joint Session is what permitted their trespass.

But who would arrest these trespassers at the White House and One Observatory Circle, the residences of the President and Vice President respectively, their presences elsewhere being permitted to them in exercise of their first Amendment right as people who would peacefully assemble to petition the Government for redress of grievances?

Citizens? *Citizens* are authorized to arrest anyone they observe committing a crime in most jurisdictions throughout the World. That includes the District of Columbia, wherein both Biden and Harris reside as *fake* President, and *fake* Vice President. DC Code § 23–582 so provides as follows.

***

(b) A private person may arrest another —
(1) who he has probable cause to believe is
committing in his presence —
(A) a felony; or
(B) an offense enumerated in section 23-
581(a)(2)[those relevant hereto being: assault,
unlawful entry, malicious destruction or injury of
another's property];

***

(c) Any person making an arrest pursuant to this section shall deliver the person arrested to a law enforcement officer without unreasonable delay.

Consequences of Biden's Impeachment

As either Biden impeachment path leads to the Constitutionally ineligible Kamala Harris ascending illegally to the Presidency, neither is an appropriate path without her inclusion in the impeachments so to preclude her ascension.

However, even if Kamala Harris could be included, and that seems unlikely absent her involvement in the impeachable offenses, absence being the defining characteristic of her Vice Presidency, the consequence would be the ascension of the current Speaker of the House, Kevin McCarthy, who is eligible to be President under the Constitution as a 'natural born Citizen' by virtue of his birth in the United States to parents who were United States Citizens at the time of his birth.

But how to remove Kamala Harris from McCarthy's path? Were Harris proven to be at the strings as Biden's puppet master, she could be impeached along with him for the Afghan Debacle. No other legal way seems available. The Congress could rescind its acceptance of the Electoral College vote. But this is so unlikely given that Harris would be presiding, albeit illegitimately, if the same procedure as for acceptance were followed. Even though there is no mandated Constitutional or other provision for rescission, however, that act may be deemed tantamount to the same process as for recording the votes of the Electors and therefore need her participation. Presumably, the Congress can rescind its prior actions by passing laws to do so. It is not clear whether this could result in the nullification of their prior acceptance of the results of the Electoral College which resulted in Biden/Harris' placement in the offices of President and Vice President.

As the consequence of such rescission would be the restoration of Trump/Pence, the rescission would not be a viable course for the Democrats.

The only other legal method would be court action, ultimately the ruling of the Supreme Court, that Harris is not a 'natural born Citizen' so Constitutionally Ineligible. Would McCarthy have standing to assert that? Would any citizen? Probably not. Probably no one other than Trump and Pence.[12] Again, since the consequence would be the restoration of Trump/Pence that is not a viable path for the Democrats either.

So the only viable legal courses of action for the Democrats and Republicans alike would seem to be the amendment processes set forth herein. As explained herein also, the alternatives, Tribal do-nothing inaction, and doomed removal procedures will prove to be divisive and destructive of Institutions, Parties, the Constitution, leading to disfunction, perhaps even assassinations and revol-utions.

Consequences of Tribal Do-nothing Inaction.

We have seen some of the consequences already.

"HOUSTON ! WE HAVE A PROBLEM!!! No this isn't a call from the space station. Texas is being invaded WITH PERMISSION FROM OUR PRESIDENT! **[Ahem! Biden is not Constitutionally President. He is a Usurper.] Texas border town makes deal with Biden administration to ship illegals to big cities. The border city's Democratic Mayor Pete Saenz said 'Border Patrol is not testing the people it is releasing for COVID before they are bused out.'"** By Bethany Blankley

"Laredo, Texas reached an agreement Wednesday to settle its lawsuit against the Biden Department of Homeland Security for transporting illegal immigrants from the Rio Grande Valley sector into the border city. Now these individuals are being transported instead to Austin, Dallas and Houston after they are released by Border Patrol. Laredo Mayor Pete Saenz, a Democrat, said Border Patrol is not testing the people it is releasing for COVID before they are bused out. Under the new agreement, the city is not required to test them, so they don't have to provide care.

"The reason why we don't do testing is that once you test, there's an obligation," Saenz told MyRGV.com. *"If they're positive, we're told that you have to quarantine. We don't have the infrastructure for that. What we're doing is coordinating with the EMC, the emergency management coordinators, in Austin and Houston, and I believe even Dallas, too ... Then, it's really up to them to continue offering PPEs, masks, hygiene, whatever they require."*

Laredo was forced to temporary shutdown after illegal immigrants created a COVID-19 outbreak, Saenz said.

"Border Patrol was very clear that they were just going to put them out in the street, in our plazas," Saenz said. *"And of course, we couldn't have that. I know some people may say, 'You're basically transporting untested people to other cities.' And the answer is, 'Yes.' But what alternative do we have here, locally?*

"At this point, we've had zero ICU beds in the last seven days. We've had people in overflow, basically waiting for a hospital bed out in the hallways. I think today we had close to 40 just waiting for a room."

"Laredo taxpayers have spent roughly $54,000 on busing out illegal immigrants so far," Saenz said.

" President **[sic]** Biden 'is letting all these people in … knowing they have COVID,' Texas Attorney General Ken Paxton told Fox News. *'They are being dropped off all over the country. I was talking to some Dallas police officers. They watched … a couple of buses unload in downtown Dallas in the middle of the night. These people just disappeared. Many of them have COVID.*

"'*And to be lectured about masks and vaccines by the administration, to be told when you are out of the country and a U.S. citizen, you can't come back if you have COVID, is hypocritical.*'" **[And also Unconstitutional.]**

"Department of Homeland Security Secretary Alejandro Mayorkas said Thursday that Border Patrol agents encountered 212,672 people who entered the southern border illegally in July, a 13% increase from the 188,000 encountered in June. [Each month ever increasing. 12/2022: 250,000.]

"Compared to the slightly more than 40,000 encountered in July 2020, the number represents a more than five-fold increase.

"The number also excludes the more than 50,000 people who evade border patrol and law enforcement every month, a conservative estimate according to border patrol officials. Mayorkas said 95,788 people were deported under Title 42, a public health protection implemented under the Trump administration. Of those not deported, according to former acting Commissioner of Customs and Border Protection Mark Morgan, Border Patrol released at least 40,000 people into the U.S. who tested positive for COVID-19.

"'*We know that everybody being released, they're not being tested,*'" Morgan said on a Zoom videomeeting sponsored by the Heritage Foundation.

"'*Let me give you another fact: 32 CBP personnel have died from COVID in the line of duty, nine in the United States Border Patrol, since the pandemic,*' Morgan added.

'Mayorkas *is directing the release of up to 80% of families who have illegally entered the United States,*" and they are not being tested for the coronavirus or other diseases, Morgan alleged.

"*We are seeing an increase in positivity rate among the migrant population,*" Mayorkas said Thursday in official remarks delivered in Brownsville, Texas. "*We built an architecture to test and isolate the migrants who make a legal claim for asylum. With respect to unaccompanied children, they are tested and cohorted on intake, before we move them as rapidly as possible to the shelter of Health and Human Services. With respect to families, we continue to operate centers where families are tested and isolated as needed. We are working and have established a system with non-governmental organizations in the communities to test and isolate, family members, as a situation warrants."*

Arizona Attorney General Mark Brnovich also expressed his consternation with the Biden administration in a recent op-ed.

"Before the Biden administration, the border had leaks," he wrote. *"Now it is broken beyond repair, and there is no doubt about the policies that have wrecked it. Border security was never intended to be a suggestion or a political lightning rod. It has real, tangible implications for all of us. Sadly, the federal government's refusal to secure the border and enforce our laws endangers public safety and deteriorates American sovereignty in ways that we have never seen."*

There is an easy solution to this problem. Send them all to the District of Columbia. The States which are now required to deal with the Dumpees should use the funds that would otherwise be required to house, feed, and medicate them to transport the Dumpees to DC. As did Laredo in sending their Dumpees on to Austin, Dallas, Houston, those cities and others of limited financial resources to the purpose could transport them to cities along the route to DC, relying on those cities to transport them evermore up the route to DC, and to finally camping out on the lawns of the White House, Number One Observatory Circle, the homes of selected Members of Congress, Senators, the Federal Judiciary, and some of the other Federal Government Officials. Meanwhile, and even thereafter, the damage that the maimed and misnamed Biden Administration hath wrought, and will, may be devastating.

Illegal Immigration. With promises of cash and other benefits, including voting rights and Citizenship, Biden has been enticing the impoverished, the terrorists, the criminals, and others from around the World, to crash the Country's Borders. In consequence, they are pouring in unregulated, infested with Covid, other diseases; mules for the illegal drug cartels; stealing, assaulting, raping; victims of others as to such; and, with Federal assistance, disappearing into the Interior, being beggared, if they are not already, and eliminated by exploitation, and other foul play. Meanwhile, there are bills pending in Congress, introduced by Democrats, and supported almost exclusively by Democrats that would legitimize illegal alien Border crashers at the expense of citizen farm workers, legitimate migrant farm workers, and immigrants generally. This is done by rewarding farmers who ignore the requirement to certify that they attempted to fill positions by hiring citizens, and failed because there were not enough to be found.

Inflation. Biden's first year in office has resulted in an inflation rate of 8.3%, the highest in 40 years. Gas price inflation is 63.9%, due primarily to Biden shutting down the pipeline from Canada to the US. This inflation was achieved without Build Back Better, which has been characterized as an inflation disaster, or an alleviator, depending on Party affiliation. It is yet to come in 2022-4 if Biden and his minions have their way! So we shall see.

Unconstitutional Regulations of State Voting Rules.
Federal. The following according to those touting the legislation. The Freedom to Vote Act is a broad package of voting, redistricting, election security, and campaign finance reforms that would ensure minimum national standards for voting access for every American. It would also prevent partisans from sabotaging election results. The John Lewis Voting Rights Advancement Act would prevent discriminatory practices and rules in voting from

being implemented in States and localities where discrimination is persistent and pervasive, protecting access to the vote for all eligible voters, regardless of race, color, or membership in language minority groups. And it would restore voters' ability to challenge discriminatory laws nationwide.

Both Acts are invasions of the States' Constitutional rights to regulate voting in their respective jurisdictions.

As Biden himself has admitted, these federal incursions on the States' Constitutional rights to manage their elections are election count acts, not voting rights acts. Fortunately, these acts have not passed. And despite Biden's stated hope that they will upon a second try, the anticipated elimination of Democrats in the 2022 and 2024 elections will provide them the decent burial that they do not deserve.

State. Additionally, there is **ranked choice voting**, a really bad idea if the voter really wants a particular candidate to win. According to rcvscam.com, the proponent is FairVote, incorporated in the District of Columbia as a domestic corporation, registered in Maryland as a foreign corporation, officed in Tacoma Park, Maryland, and funded by Soros and his minions.

So what to do? Don't play the game! Just vote for your candidate and no other. That defeats **ranked choice voting** without having to do anything more. Spread the word how to defeat **ranked choice voting** to all so that no one falls into the trap of ranked choice prevailing over one's actual choice.

Defunding the Police. As federal funding of State police is very limited, the federal impact on defunding of the police is too.[13] However, that does not mean that the Democrat Party is not heavily committed to defunding the police at all levels except federal, i.e. Capitol Police, FBI, CIA, of course. The mayors of the cities in which defunding and consequent increases in crime have already occurred--Atlanta, Austin, Baltimore, Chicago, DC, Hartford, Los Angeles, Milwaukee, Minneapolis, New York, Norman, Philadelphia, Portland, Salt Lake City, Seattle--are all Democrats. Travel to or through these jurisdictions is to be discouraged as too dangerous. Those who can are exiting. Those who must do business there are thankful for the Internet.

No Prosecution/No Bail. Biden/Harris are not to blame personally, but their Democrat Party may be for the soft-on-crime, no prosecution, no bail posture of the Soros funded Democrat Prosecutors who definitely are to blame. Among them are

Austin District Attorney Jose Garza (Soros $625,000+), Chicago DA Kim Foxx (Soros $2,300,000+), Los Angeles DA George Gascon (Soros $2,500,000+) Manhattan DA Alvin Bragg (Soros $1,000,000+), Philadelphia DA Larry Krasner (Soros: $1,700,000+), San Francisco DA Chesa Boudin (Soros: $600,000+ and $180,000 in unsuccessful defense against recall), [whose parents were members of the Weather Underground domestic terrorists][14]

Also: Florida Orange County DA Aramis Aya la (Soros $1,300,000+), her successor Monique Worrell (Soros: $1,500,000+), Hinds County Mississippi DA Jody Owens (Soros $500,000+), Columbus Mississippi DA Scott Colom (Soros $926,000+), Albuquerque New Mexico DA Raul Torrez (Soros $107,000+), Bexar County Texas DA Joe Gonzalez (Soros $1,000,000+), Dallas County Texas DA John Creuzot (Soros $236,000+), Contra Costa DA Diane Becton (Soros $275,000+), St. Louis DA Kim Gardner (Soros $116,000+), David Clegg (Soros $184,000+), County Pennsylvania DA Jack Stollsteimer (Soros $100,000+), Arlington County Virginia DA Parisa Dehghani-Tafti (Soros $600,000+), Fairfax County Virginia DA SteveDescano (Soros $600,000+), Buta Biberaj (Soros $650,000+), Ramin Fatehi (Soros $220,000+).[15]

Soros also contributed more than $500,000 to Biden, which raises the question whether foreigners should be able to contribute even indirectly, as Soros always asserts they should, to US and State candidates.

WHO IS ELIGIBLE IN 2024?

X Donald Trump is disqualified if he be deemed to have been President during the term during the 2020-2024 term which Biden usurped. This follows analytically from Biden having been disqualified because Biden had already served two prior terms due to Obama's disqualification, that being because Obama is not a 'natural born Citizen' as the Constitution requires. Elimination of the two term limitation would be required to eliminate any doubt as to Trump's qualification for re-election in 2024. Additionally, his disqualification could be eliminated by eliminating the 'natural born Citizen' requirement of the Constitution retrospectively so to legitimize Obama's Presidency.

X Joseph Biden was disqualified from being elected President in 2020 due to his having already served two terms because he was the duly elected Vice President who took the place of the disqualified Obama pursuant to the provision for such in the Constitution. Accordingly, as in 2020, Biden is currently disqualified from being legitimately elected President in 2024. Elimination of the two term limitation would be required to eliminate any doubt as to Biden's qualification for re-election in 2024. Alternatively, such doubt could be eliminated by eliminating the 'natural born Citizen' requirement of the Constitution retrospective to before Obama's first election to the Presidency so to eliminate his disqualification and Biden's resultant ascendancy.

X Kamala Harris was disqualified from being elected Vice President in 2020 because she is not a 'natural born Citizen' as required by the Constitution of one who would be Vice President. She is likewise disqualified from becoming President in 2024.

X Nikki Haley (birth name Nimrata Randhawa) was born in the United States to foreign immigrants who were ineligible for naturalization until at least a year after Nikki's birth. Accordingly, a 'natural born Citizen' she is not, and therefore not qualified to be elected President.

That she is suggesting legislation to require those 75 and older to submit to competency testing should be seen for what it is, her attacking Trump (76) and Biden (81) as a fruitless diversion from her own ineligibility. Additionally, such legislation would be unconstitutional because the qualifications for the office are set forth in the Constitution, and cannot be added to, or changed, except by amendment of the Constitution.

X Piyush "Bobby" Jindal was born in the United States to foreign immigrants who were ineligible for naturalization until about five years after his birth. Accordingly, a 'natural born Citizen' he is not, and therefore not qualified to be elected President.

X Tulsi Gabbard was born in American Samoa of parents who were both United States Citizens at the time of her birth. As such, she has a problem unique among those who would be Presidential Candidates in 2024. Americans born in that territory have US nationality but not US citizenship. The local government and people so far have not petitioned Congress for US citizen status. But those born there to US citizen parents acquire parental citizenship at birth.

While American Samoa is a "territory" of the United States, it is not an "incorporated territory." *Downes v. Bidwell, 182 U.S. 244 (1901)* held that unincorporated territories, even if under the control of the United States, are not, prior to formal action by Congress, a part of the United States.

Rassmussen v. United States, 197 U.S. 516 (1905) held that the full spectrum of the Constitution's provisions apply only in incorporated territories of the United States, thereby excluding from that full spectrum its application in unincorporated territories.

This conclusion is also fortified by recognition that, after enacting 1 Stat. 103, the "1790 Naturalization Act," declaring children born to US citizen parents "beyond sea" (i.e., not in the United States) to be "considered" natural born citizens, Congress repealed altogether that law by enacting 1 Stat. 414 in 1795, the "1795 Naturalization Act." The new law provided that such children were to be "considered" only US citizens, not natural born Citizens. The title of the 1795 Act was: "An Act to establish an uniform rule of Naturalization; and to repeal the act heretofore passed on that subject."

Not only the facts above but the fact that she obtained her citizenship by an act of Congress makes her a naturalized citizen, not a Natural Born Citizen.

This falls in line with 8USC1401 of the of the Immigration and Nationality Act of 1952. It provides as follows.

"Nationals and citizens of United States at birth

"The following shall be nationals and citizens of the United States at birth:

***

"(c) a person born outside of the United States and its outlying possessions of parents both of whom are citizens of the United States and one of whom has had a residence in the United States or one of its outlying possessions, prior to the birth of such person."

This makes Gabbard a naturalized citizen if her parents followed the directions of the State Department. She is not a 'natural born Citizen'.

Luria v. United States, 231 U.S. 9 (1913), states: "Citizenship is membership in a political society, and implies a duty of allegiance on the part of the member and a duty of protection on the part of the society. These are reciprocal obligations, one being a compensation for the other. Under our Constitution, a naturalized citizen stands on an equal footing with the native citizen in all respects save that of eligibility to the Presidency. *Minor v. Happersett, 88 U. S. 165 (1874); Elk v. Wilkins, 112 U. S. 94, 112 U. S. 101 (1884); Osborn v. Bank of United States, 22 U. S. 827 (1824).*"

Since Gabbard was not born in the US, she cannot be a 'natural born Citizen'.

Since Gabbard was not born in any State, she has no US birth Certificate issued by any State to prove her citizenship.

Gabbard should have a CRBA (certificate of birth abroad) or a Form FS-240 since she was not born in a State of the United States that could issue a birth

certificate. Her parents should have contacted either the US Embassy or US Consulate to report the birth and acquire the document. They did not. (https://uscode.house.gov/view.xhtml?path=/preli m@title8/chapter12/subchapter3&edition=prelim) From the US State Department:
"Birth of U.S. Citizens Abroad:
"A child born abroad to a U.S. citizen parent or parents may acquire U.S. citizenship at birth if certain statutory requirements are met. The child's parents should contact the nearest U.S. embassy or consulate to apply for a Consular Report of Birth Abroad of a Citizen of the United States of America (CRBA) to document that the child is a U.S. citizen. If the U.S. embassy or consulate determines that the child acquired U.S. citizenship at birth, a consular officer will approve the CRBA application and the Department of State will issue a CRBA, also called a Form FS-240, in the child's name."
In *United States V. Wong Kim Ark, 169 US 649* (1898), the Supreme Court said this:
"…A person born out of the jurisdiction of the United States can only become a citizen by being naturalized, either by treaty, as in the case of the annexation of foreign territory, or by authority of Congress, exercised either by declaring certain classes of persons to be citizens, as in the enactments conferring citizenship upon foreign-

born children of citizens, or by enabling foreigners individually to become citizens…"

That Gabbard was not born in America disqualifies her becoming President despite her parents both being US Citizens at her birth. She cannot even establish that she is a US citizen. Perhaps, like Ted Cruz, she is an illegal alien. May Gabbard herself resolve her citizenship problems other than her not being a 'natural born Citizen' by now seeking a CRBA or FS-240. Apparently not, as the application for such must be made by the subject's 18th birthday. She should not also that the form scheme for such is all screwed up.

X Marco Rubio is disqualified from being President because he is not a 'natural born Citizen' due to his parents not having been US Citizens, even though in the US, and even though Rubio was born in the US.

√ **Hillary Clinton** is qualified because she is a 'natural born citizen' and she is not constrained by the two term limit.

X William Clinton is disqualified because he has already served two terms; but he would be qualified were that limitation removed by amendment of the Constitution timely to the 2024 election.

X Ted Cruz is disqualified because he was born in Canada of parents who were not US Citizens.

Despite his having renounced his Canadian Citizenship in 2014, he is not even a US Citizen in that he has never gone through the required naturalization process. Therefore, he is an illegal alien, and not even Constitutionally qualified to be a Senator.

X Andrew Yang appears to be disqualified because his immigrant parents appear never to have applied for, nor obtained US Citizenship even though they and Yang were in the United States at his birth.

The following other potential candidates may be free from all of the Constitutional disqualifications that plague the foregoing.

√ **Ron DeSantis** is Constitutionally qualified in that he was born in the United States of parents who were United States Citizens at the time of his birth.

√ **Michael Pence** is qualified to be elected President in 2024 because he is a 'natural born Citizen' and he does not suffer a two term limitation, there being no limit to the number of terms a Vice President may serve as such, it having no effect on terms of office as President. One must keep in mind, however, that at the 2023 annual DC Gridiron Dinner Pence did misstate: "I had no right to overturn the election. And [Trump's] words endangered my family and everyone at the Capitol that day. And I know that history will hold Donald Trump accountable." To the contrary, Pence did have such right. Due to Pence's inaction, illegitimate electors were able to cause Biden's third term as President, Harris to become Vice President, both in violation of the Constitution, all as highlighted and explained hereinbefore. History will subscribe Pence to everlasting bonfire of infamy for his refusal to do the right thing. His only excuses may be his ignorance and stupidity, which should be characteristics sufficient to disqualify him from even being considered for the Presidency.

? Vivek Ramaswamy is qualified if his father was a US citizen at the time of Vivek's birth in Cleveland, Ohio in 1985. If elected, he would be the youngest President ever, although not the youngest to ever run, that being the honor of William Jennings Bryant at 36. Harold Stassen's first run was at 37 Theodore Roosevelt was the youngest to become President. He was 42 when as Vice President, he succeeded to the Presidency upon the assassination of William McKinley. The youngest to be elected President was John F. Kennedy at 43.

√ Marianne Williamson is not disqualified from the Office of the President. She is an author and lecturer. All her prior efforts for elective office have failed.

ONLY 4 OF THE 15 MOST LIKELY TO RUN FOR PRESIDENT ARE CONSTITUTIONALLY QUALIFED TO DO SO.
A SAD COMMENTARY!
THIS MUST BE CAUSING THE FOUNDING FATHERS TO BE TURNING IN THEIR GRAVES…WHAT HAS THE COUNTRY COME TO???

FOOTNOTES

[1]*A (sic) Historian Told Us Why Woodrow Wilson Was the Worst U.S. President Ever*, Robert W. Merry, The National Interest, 7/3/2020. Is Biden replacing Wilson as the Worst? Not if Biden is not Constitutionally the President. Trump the worst because he threw his lunch against the wall when Barr announced there was no evidence of fraud in the 2020 Election? Barf!!! The frauds were staring everyone in the face and they did not recognize them—*Third Term* Biden and *Not Natural Born Harris*!!! For which see the next footnote.

[2]Vattel, *The Law of Nations*, Book II, Chapter XIX: "§212. The citizens are the. members of the civil society; bound. to this society by certain duties, and subject to its authority, they equally participate in its advantages. **The natives, or natural-born citizens, are those born in the country, of parents who are citizens.** As the society cannot exist and perpetuate itself otherwise than by the children of the citizens, those children naturally follow the condition of their fathers, and succeed to all their rights. The society is supposed to desire this, in consequence of what it owes to its own preservation; and it is presumed, as matter of course, that each citizen, on entering into society, reserves to his children the right of becoming members of it. The country of the fathers. is therefore that of the children; and these become true citizens merely by their tacit consent. We shall soon see whether, on their coming to the years of discretion, they may renounce their right, and what they owe to the society in which they were born. I say, that, **in order to be of the country, it is necessary that a person be born of a father who is a citizen; for, if he is born there of a foreigner, it will be only the place of his birth, and not his country.**

"§213. The inhabitants, as distinguished from citizens, are foreigners who are permitted to settle and stay in the country. Bound to the society by the residence, they are subject to the laws of the state while they reside in it; and they are obliged to defend it, because it grants them protection, though they do not participate in all the rights of citizens. They enjoy only the advantages which the law or custom gives them. The perpetual inhabitants are those who have received the, right of perpetual residence. These are a kind of citizens of an inferior order, and are united to the society without participating in all its advantages. Their children follow the condition of their fathers; and as the state has given to these the right of perpetual residence, their right passes to their posterity,

"§214. A nation, or the sovereign who represents it, may grant to a foreigner the quality of citizen, by admitting him into the body of the political society. This is called naturalization. There are some states in which the sovereign cannot grant to a foreigner all the rights of citizens, for example, that of holding public offices, and where, consequently, he has the power of granting only an imperfect naturalization. It is here a regulation of the fundamental law, which limits the power of the prince. In other states, as in England and Poland, the prince cannot naturalize a single person, without the concurrence of the nation represented by its deputies. Finally, there are states, as, for instance, England where the single circumstance of being born in the country, naturalizes the children of a foreigner.

"§215. It is asked whether the children born of citizens in a foreign country are citizens? The laws have decided this question in several countries, and their regulations must be followed. By the law of nature alone, children follow the condition of their fathers, and enter into all their rights (§212); the place of birth produces no change in this particular, and cannot, of itself, furnish any reason for taking from a child what nature has given him; I say "of itself," for, civil or political laws may, for particular reasons, ordain otherwise. But I suppose that the father has not entirely quitted his country in order to settle elsewhere. If he has fixed his abode in a foreign country he is 'become a member of another society, at least as its perpetual inhabitant; and his children will be members of it also."

[3]From Speech given at the Text and Teaching Symposium, Georgetown University, 10/12/85..

[4]Saving President Trump's Second Term

Gregory Cliveden

https://www.amazon.com/dp/B08Q4L8DB9
THERE YOU WILL FIND: *The Conventioneers'*

Guide to the Party at the End of Its Universe. The advice therein for VP Mike Pence, Rudy Giuliani, and the minions assuring Trump/Pence another four years is extremely time sensitive. You must read and act immediately. The Electors met in their respective States 12/14. Their meetings and votes should have been enjoined in tandem, separately, and otherwise as needed with Rudy's fraud claims, but that did not occur, even though I sent the message to the appropriate persons. Pence must now follow the instructions of *The Conventioneers' Guide to the Party at the End of Its Universe* to assure that the Biden/ Harris Elect- oral Votes are not received or counted and that only the Electoral Votes for Trump /Pence, and any miscellaneous other qualified Candidates are the only ones counted.

As explained at much greater length and detail in *The Conventioneers' Guide to the Party at the End of Its Universe*, the premise for Pence as President of the Senate presiding over the JOINT SESSION of Congress not accepting the Biden /Harris Certifications and their ballots for Electoral Vote count is that Biden has already served Two Terms, and cannot Constitutionally serve a Third Term. His two prior terms are the result of Obama having been Constitutionally ineligible for the Office of President because his Father was a British Subject at the time of Obama's birth. Therefore, whether he was born in Hawaii or not, he is not a 'natural born Citizen' within its meaning at the time of the drafting of the Constitution.

A Vice President assumes the Presidency in such a circumstance. Harris, of course, suffers the same ineligibility as Obama. Her father was a British Subject at the time of her birth. Although he did become a naturalized US citizen later, that is irrelevant to determining 'natural born Citizen' status. This is elucidated in *The Conventioneers' Guide to the Party at the End of Its Universe*. Although the eligibility issues as to Obama, Biden, and Harris are commented upon throughout, the best, and most thorough summaries are set forth therein beginning with *Why Can't Biden be President?* and continuing through to the end of *that book*. ***Why Can't Biden be President? (p. 738 in the paperback)/Why Can't Harris be Vice President? (p.740)/"What is to be Done?": Biden/Harris (p.741)/ Trump/Pence (p.743) /Legal Underpinning (p.747/ Potential for Dire Consequences (p.755).***

Trump/Pence would have entered upon their entitled four more years in the offices of President and Vice President, respectively, had the courses of action set forth in that book been followed. This appeared to be the only way, even if Rudy were somewhat successful with ballot box fraud litigation. As the President asked in another context: "What have you got to lose?" I did what I could to get this message to Pence. The health of the Nation under the Constitution depended on it. And Its health otherwise as well, as we are seeing under Biden/Harris. Gregory Cliveden.]

[5]This date would obviate any question about Obama's eligibility. However, any amendment prior to the 2024 election would probably suffice to include him, Bush, and Clinton too. Obama's eligibility, of course, would require redefinition of 'natural born Citizen' too.

What about the States? As an alternative, the State Legislatures may apply to Congress for a Convention to make the Amendment. That too requires a 2/3rds vote, but without the ambiguity between both and each. Currently, there are 50 States. So 2/3rds would be 34 States. Assuming a vote along Party lines, neither Party could effect such an Application because the Republicans have 31 of the State Legislatures and the Democrats 18, even with Democrats Manchin and Sinema voting as if Republicans. Approving the Amendment at the Convention called either way would be even more unlikely because 3/4ths of the State Legislatures would have to vote in favor.

[6]Possible currently is an interminable Vice President, and a puppet two term President, a more

perpetual scheme than keeps Russia's Putin in perpetual power.

[7]This date is necessary to eliminate Obama's ineligibility, and to create Biden's eligibility for a third term, in the event an AMENDMENT XXVIII is not timely adopted.

[8]To date, Congress has not done so.

[9]Farrand's Records of the Constitutional Convention, pp.550-1. Col. Mason. "Why is the provision restrained to Treason & bribery only? Treason as defined in the Constitution will not reach many great and dangerous offences. Hastings is not guilty of Treason. Attempts to subvert the Constitution may not be Treason as above defined— As bills of attainder which have saved the British Constitution are forbidden, it is the more necessary to extend: the power of impeachments." He moved. to add after bribery *or maladministration*. Mr. Gerry seconded him—
Mr. Madison: "So vague a term will be equivalent to a tenure during pleasure of the Senate." Mr. Govr Morris: "It will not be put in force & can do no harm— An election of every four years will prevent maladministration." Col. Mason withdrew "maladministration" & substitutes "other high crimes & misdemeanors" ⟨agst. the State"⟩ 7 On

the question thus altered N. H— ay. Mas. ay— Ct. ay. ⟨N. J. no⟩ Pa no. Del. no. Md ay. Va. ay. N. C. ay. S. C. ay.* Geo. ay. [Ayes — 8; noes — 3.]

[10]Impeachable Offenses: Historical Background | Constitution Annotated | Congress.gov | Library of Congress: "At the time of ratification of the Constitution, the phrase "high crimes and misdemeanors" thus appears understood to have applied to uniquely "political" offenses, or misdeeds committed by public officials against the state. Alexander Hamilton, in explaining the Constitution's impeachment provisions, described impeachable offenses as arising from "the misconduct of public men, or in other words from the abuse or violation of some public trust." Such offenses were "Political, as they relate chiefly to injuries done immediately to the society itself."[a] In the centuries following the Constitution's ratification, precisely what behavior constitutes a high crime or misdemeanor has been the subject of much debate."[b]

[a]The Federalist No. 65 (Alexander Hamilton)

[b]*Compare* H.R. Rep. No. 105-830, at 110–18 (1998) (majority views), *with id.* at 204 (minority views). *See* Gary L. McDowell, *High Crimes and Misdemeanors: Recovering the Intentions of the Founders,* 67 Geo. Wash. L. Rev. 626, 627 (1999); Laurence H. Tribe, *Defining High Crimes*

and Misdemeanors: Basic Principles, 67 Geo. Wash. L. Rev. 712, 717 (1999).

[11]For analysis of standing, see fn3 above, and *The Conventioneers' Guide to the Party at the End of Its Universe*, pp.741-754.

[12]In FY21, the Department of Labor (DOL) certified over 317,000 seasonal farm jobs to be filled by H-2A workers, up 15 percent from 275,000 in FY20. About 80 percent of H-2A jobs that were certified resulted in the issuance of H-2A visas, some 258,000 in FY21, including a peak 40,000 in March, 36,000 in April, and 34,000 in May. These three months accounted for 110,000 or 43 percent of H-2A visas issued.

The Farm Workforce Modernization Act, approved by the House in March 2021, would legalize unauthorized farm workers. Barriers to H-2A workers would be reduced and dairy and other year-round farm jobs would be open to H-2A workers for the first time.

DOL certifies employers to fill over 97 percent of the jobs they want to fill with H-2A workers. H-2A workers are in the US an average of six months, which means they filled about 125,000 year-round equivalent jobs, 11 percent of the 1.1 million full time equivalent jobs in US crop agriculture. Over half of H-2A jobs are in five states: California,

Florida, Georgia, North Carolina, and Washington. The share of H-2A jobs in these five States rose from 34 percent in 2007 to 52 percent in 2021 due to the growth in each State and especially in California and Washington, States where the number of jobs certified rose by 14-fold and 15-fold, respectively.

As the Congressional debate continues, more farm employers (including labor contractors) are building housing in order to employ H-2A workers. At the same time, sharp increases in farm labor costs are accelerating efforts to change farming systems in ways that facilitate labor-saving mechanization and encouraging more imports of fresh fruits and vegetables from abroad, especially from Mexico, the source of half of US fresh fruit and three-fourths of US fresh vegetable imports.

Pending for consideration by the House is H. R. 1603. It provides for certifying agricultural worker status and changing the H-2A temporary worker program.

The Department of Homeland Security (DHS) may grant certified agricultural worker (CAW) status to an alien who (1) performed at least 1,035 hours of agricultural labor during the two-year period prior to March 8, 2021; (2) on that date was inadmissible, deportable, or under a grant of deferred enforced departure or temporary protected status; and (3) has been continuously present in the United States from that date until receiving CAW status. The bill imposes additional crime-related inadmissibility grounds on CAW applicants and makes some other grounds inapplicable.

CAW status shall be valid for 5.5 years and may be extended. DHS may grant dependent status to the spouse or children of a principal alien.

An alien with a pending application may not be detained or removed by DHS and shall be authorized for employment until DHS makes a final decision on the application.

A CAW alien (and dependents) may apply for lawful permanent resident status after meeting various requirements, including performing a certain amount of agricultural labor for a number of years.

DHS is to create an electronic platform for (1) filing H-2A petitions, (2) facilitating the processing of H-2A cases, and (3) providing agencies a single tool for obtaining H-2A-related case information.

The bill makes various changes to the H-2A program, such as (1) modifying the method for calculating and making adjustments to the H-2A worker minimum wage, (2) specifying how an employer may satisfy requirements that it attempted to recruit U.S. workers, (3) requiring H-2A employers to guarantee certain minimum work hours, (4) making the program available for agricultural work that is not temporary or seasonal, and (5) reserving a visa allocation for the dairy industry.

DHS is to establish a pilot program allowing certain H-2A workers to apply for portable status, which gives the worker 60 days after leaving a position to secure new employment with a registered H-2A employer.

DHS is to establish an electronic system patterned on the E-Verify Program for employers to verify an individual's identity and employment authorization. Employers hiring individuals for agricultural employment must use the system.

This bill permanently establishes the Housing Preservation and Revitalization Program, which provides financing assistance for rural rental housing and off-farm labor housing and rental assistance for qualified tenants of such housing. It also authorizes the Department of Agriculture to provide various assistance, including funding for insuring loans and grants for new farmworker housing.

[13]See *Federal(De)Funding of Local Police*, 110 Georgetown Law Journal, Summer '21.

[14]From **How George Soros funded progressive 'legal arsonist' DAs behind US crime surge**, by Isabel Vincent, New York Post 12/16/2021.

[15]From **Living Room Pundit's Guide to Soros District Attorneys** by Parker Thayer, Capital Research Center, Capital Research.org. 1/18/2022.

~

DID NOT HAPPEN.
THE IDIOC Y CONTINUED!!!

TOO MANY IDIOTS IGNORANT OF THE
CONSTITUTIONAL REQUIREMENTS
FOR PRESIDENT!!!
HOPEFULLY, THEY ARE EDUCABLE,
THIS WILL BE CORRECTED, AND THIS
WILL NOT HAPPEN AGAIN!!!